The editors would like to thank
TOM DI LIBERTO,
climate scientist, National Oceanic and Atmospheric Administration,
for his assistance in the preparation of this book.

Visit us on the Web!
Seussville.com
rhcbooks.com

Educators and librarians, for a variety of teaching tools, visit us at RHTeachersLibrarians.com

Library of Congress Cataloging-in-Publication Data is available upon request.
ISBN 978-0-593-43383-6 (trade) — ISBN 978-0-593-43384-3 (lib. bdg.)

MANUFACTURED IN CHINA

10 9 8 7 6 5 4 3 2 1

First Edition

WACKY WEATHER

by Todd Tarpley

illustrated by Aristides Ruiz and Alan Batson

The Cat in the Hat's Learning Library®

Random House 🏠 New York

You probably know
about rain, sleet, and snow,
thunder and lightning,
and strong winds that blow.

You may know that summer
is warmer than fall—
but that is not all!
Oh, no, that is not all!

Some weather's so odd
that you'd swear it can't be.
If you want to learn more,
then come on! Follow me!

I'm the Cat in the Hat,
and we'll travel together
to learn about all kinds
of weird, wacky weather!

First, a trip to the Arctic,
and as we pass by,
we will get a close look
at strange lights in the sky.

Aurora borealis
or just northern lights—
whatever you call them,
they're curious sights!

They're caused when small particles
blown by the sun
collide with Earth's atmosphere—
oh, my! What fun!

Aurora Borealis

The most common color
is yellowish-green,
but pink, red, and purple
have also been seen.

This next odd occurrence
may give you a jolt:
it's lightning that comes in a ball,
not a bolt!

Ball Lightning

Instead of a strike
it just floats in the air.
Few people have seen one,
which makes it quite rare.

In fact, this strange lightning
that looks like a ball
may not even REALLY
be lightning at all!

What causes these balls, then?
Well, no one can say.
But until we find out,
we'll stay out of the way!

Calling all earthlings!

Shout it out loud!

This huge flying saucer

IS ONLY A CLOUD!

Lenticular Cloud

Moist air hits a mountain,
becoming unsteady.
It rises and falls,
then swirls up in an eddy.

It forms a strange cloud
as it starts to ascend.
It isn't a spaceship—
but we can pretend!

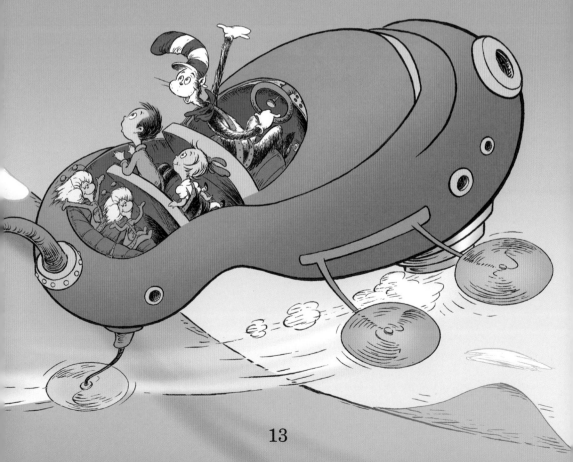

Now, speaking of clouds,

here is one that is scary.

Does it look like a giant tsunami?

Yes, very!

It's usually found

out in front of a storm.

Moist, rising air helps

a shelf cloud to form.

Shelf Cloud

The cloud is quite harmless.
Beware anyhow:
a storm will be coming
so get inside NOW!

This long, skinny cloud
is round, like a pole.
It looks like a white-frosted
cinnamon roll.

Roll Cloud

We call it a roll cloud,
but let me repeat it—
although it looks tasty,
you can't really eat it.

If you think that was wacky,
here's one even odder.
It's like a tornado—
but over the water!

Waterspout

Waterspouts stir up
the water they touch,
but they don't suck it up
(at least not very much).

Fish Rain?

Could a waterspout suck up
fish into the air?
When the wind settles down,
there'd be fish everywhere!

In the streets, on the roofs,
onto folks passing by!
"Look!" they'd say. "It's
raining FISH from the sky!"

Yet no one has really
seen "fish rain" occur.
So it may not be true.
(But we wish that it were!)

Though some say "firenado,"
tornadoes they're not.
Both have a funnel shape.
Both spin a lot.

But unlike tornadoes,
which form way up high,
a fire whirl forms
on the ground, not the sky.

Fire Whirl

They usually start from
a wildfire that's burning.
The wind whips it into
a funnel that's churning.

They don't rise too high,
and they don't last too long.
But they're still very dangerous.
Let's move along!

These LOOK like tornadoes
but tend to be small—
a few feet around
and not terribly tall.

Dust devils do NOT come
from clouds in a storm.
They need hot, sunny weather
in order to form.

You see them in deserts
and other dry places.
They don't last too long,
but please cover your faces!

Dust Devil

Here's one final whirl
that you really should know.
It's called a snownado—
it's made out of snow!

Snownado

It's NOT a tornado—
I think you know why.
It forms on the ground
and not up in the sky.

Sounds like a fire whirl
or dust devil, right?
Exactly, but quite
a bit colder—and white!

It's time for some donuts!
But don't be too hasty.
They're made out of snow,
so they won't be too tasty!

When the snow in a tree
gets too heavy, it drops.
It lands on the ground
where it usually stops.

And yet, now and then,
if the wind is just right,
the snow starts to roll
until—done!—take a bite.

Snow Donut

Hailstones, you know,
are just small balls of ice.
But if they grow larger?
Look out—they're not nice!

They start as small droplets
of water, not snow.
The stronger the wind blows,
the larger they grow.

They freeze in the updraft.
They fall and they rise.
Until they're too heavy
to stay in the skies.

Giant Hailstones

They can grow to the size
of a coconut—true!
I'd prefer not to be underneath.
Wouldn't you?

This next one might make you cry,
"I want my mommy!"
if you should encounter
a rare ice tsunami!

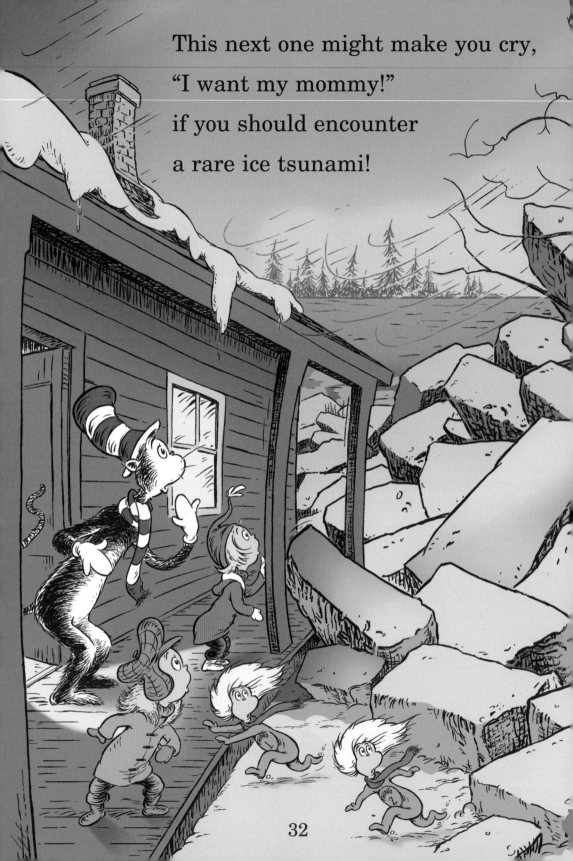

When ice on a lake
starts to melt after winter,
the wind starts to blow
and the slabs start to splinter.

Ice Tsunami

A strong wind can push them
right onto the shore.
Imagine this huge
wall of ice at your door!

Red sprites are large flashes
of light in the sky.
They occur in the atmosphere
FIFTY MILES HIGH!

Red Sprites

They form above storms,
where they flicker and glow.
They seem to be triggered
by lightning below.

You'd better look fast
when they come into view.
Red sprites only last
a split second or two!

Why, it looks like three suns!

Are we on a strange planet?

Surely this can't be a real thing—
or can it?

Sun Dog

Sun dogs appear

when the sun is down low,

when there's ice in the clouds

(and sometimes when there's snow).

The ice in the clouds
refracts light, as you see.
Instead of one sun,
well, it looks like there's three!

There's weird, wacky weather
all over the place.
Not only on Earth,
but even in space!

Jupiter's Great Red Spot

On Jupiter,
there is a storm that's so wide,
that two or three Earths
would fit snugly inside!

On Neptune, the rain would be
hard to walk through.
It's not made of water,
but diamonds—it's true!

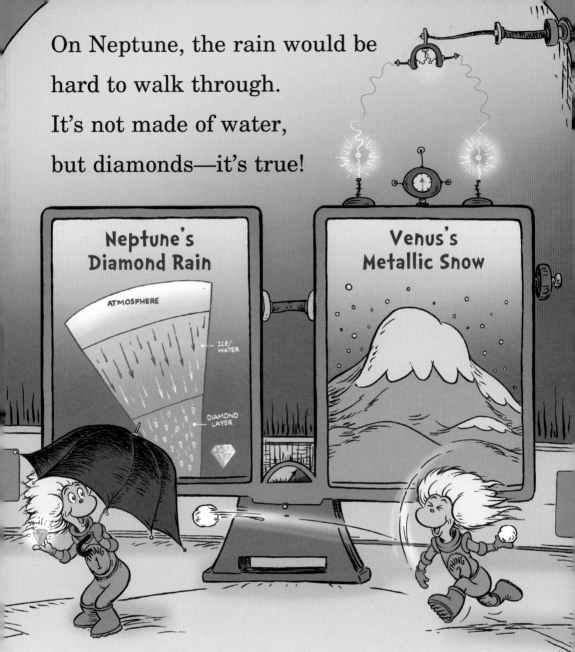

Neptune's
Diamond Rain

ATMOSPHERE

ICE/
WATER

DIAMOND
LAYER

Venus's
Metallic Snow

And on Venus, there's snow
made of metal, not ice!
(Getting hit with a snowball
there wouldn't be nice.)

Thank you for joining
this field trip together.
I would've enjoyed it
in all kinds of weather!

But now that we're home,
well, I'm happy to say—
here comes the sunshine.
Let's go out and play!

GLOSSARY

Arctic: The area near the North Pole. It includes areas of land, ocean, and ice.

Ascend: To rise through the air.

Atmosphere: The gases surrounding a planet.

Aurora borealis: A natural light display near the Arctic regions, also known as northern lights. Near the Antarctic regions they are known as aurora australis.

Bolt: A flash of lightning.

Churning: Swirling quickly and violently.

Collide: To smash into.

Earthlings: How an alien might refer to humans. It is popular in science-fiction books and movies, but it is not a word used by scientists.

Eddy: A circular, swirling movement of water or air.

Funnel: The shape of an ice cream cone, wide at the top and narrow at the bottom. A tornado is called a funnel cloud because of its shape.

Jolt: A sudden and violent shock, like being struck by lightning. It could also mean a less dangerous kind of shock, like being suddenly surprised.

Occurrence: Anything that happens.

Particles: Tiny pieces of matter and energy, like atoms.

Refraction: The way light bends as it passes through water or ice.

Sleet: Small pellets of ice often mixed with rain and snow.

Tsunami: A huge wave—or several in a row—caused by landslides, earthquakes, and even the eruption of underwater volcanoes.

Updraft: An upward current of air.

Wacky: Weird or strange.

FOR FURTHER READING

Clouds by Anne Rockwell, illustrated by Frané Lessac (HarperCollins, Let's-Read-and-Find-Out Science, Stage 1). An easy-to-read book about different types of clouds from an award-winning nonfiction series. Includes instructions to make your own cloud! For preschool and up.

Cloudy with a Chance of Meatballs by Judi Barrett, illustrated by Ron Barrett (Atheneum Books for Young Readers). A beloved—and very funny—picture book about a town where food rains down from the sky and how people cope with it. For preschool and up.

Lightning by Seymour Simon (HarperCollins). An introduction to lightning by an award-winning science writer, illustrated with dramatic, colorful photographs. Other books in the same series include *Hurricanes, Storms,* and *Weather.* For grades 1 and up.

SkySisters by Jan Bourdeau Waboose, illustrated by Brian Deines (Kids Can Press). An award-winning picture book about two Ojibway sisters who set off on a wintry night to see the northern lights, or SkySpirits, who dance in the sky. For kindergarten and up.

INDEX